Put Beginning Readers on the Right Track with ALL ABOARD READING™

The All Aboard Reading series is especially designed for beginning readers. Written by noted authors and illustrated in full color, these are books that children really want to read—books to excite their imagination, expand their interests, make them laugh, and support their feelings. With fiction and nonfiction stories that are high interest and curriculum-related, All Aboard Reading books offer something for every young reader. And with four different reading levels, the All Aboard Reading series lets you choose which books are most appropriate for your children and their growing abilities.

Picture Readers
Picture Readers have super-simple texts, with many nouns appearing as rebus pictures. At the end of each book are 24 flash cards—on one side is a rebus picture; on the other side is the written-out word.

Station Stop 1
Station Stop 1 books are best for children who have just begun to read. Simple words and big type make these early reading experiences more comfortable. Picture clues help children to figure out the words on the page. Lots of repetition throughout the text helps children to predict the next word or phrase—an essential step in developing word recognition.

Station Stop 2
Station Stop 2 books are written specifically for children who are reading with help. Short sentences make it easier for early readers to understand what they are reading. Simple plots and simple dialogue help children with reading comprehension.

Station Stop 3
Station Stop 3 books are perfect for children who are reading alone. With longer text and harder words, these books appeal to children who have mastered basic reading skills. More complex stories captivate children who are ready for more challenging books.

In addition to All Aboard Reading books, look for All Aboard Math Readers™ (fiction stories that teach math concepts children are learning in school); All Aboard Science Readers™ (nonfiction books that explore the most fascinating science topics in age-appropriate language); All Aboard Poetry Readers™ (funny, rhyming poems for readers of all levels); and All Aboard Mystery Readers™ (puzzling tales where children piece together evidence with the characters).

All Aboard for happy reading!

For Allie, the Yankee fan in the family.

GROSSET & DUNLAP
Published by the Penguin Group
Penguin Group (USA) Inc., 375 Hudson Street, New York, New York 10014, USA
Penguin Group (Canada), 90 Eglinton Avenue East, Suite 700, Toronto, Ontario M4P 2Y3, Canada
(a division of Pearson Penguin Canada Inc.)
Penguin Books Ltd., 80 Strand, London WC2R 0RL, England
Penguin Group Ireland, 25 St. Stephen's Green, Dublin 2, Ireland
(a division of Penguin Books Ltd.)
Penguin Group (Australia), 250 Camberwell Road, Camberwell, Victoria 3124, Australia
(a division of Pearson Australia Group Pty. Ltd.)
Penguin Books India Pvt. Ltd., 11 Community Centre, Panchsheel Park, New Delhi—110 017, India
Penguin Group (NZ), 67 Apollo Drive, Rosedale, North Shore 0632, New Zealand
(a division of Pearson New Zealand Ltd.)
Penguin Books (South Africa) (Pty.) Ltd., 24 Sturdee Avenue,
Rosebank, Johannesburg 2196, South Africa

Penguin Books Ltd., Registered Offices:
80 Strand, London WC2R 0RL, England

Photo credits: cover: Al Bello/Getty Images; copyright page: Lisa Blumenfeld/Getty Images; title
page: John Williamson/MLB Photos via Getty Images; page 6: Timothy A. Clary/AFP/Getty Images;
page 9: AP Images; page 12: Rich Pilling/MLB Photos; page 13: Getty Images for Madame Tussauds;
page 16: AP Photo/Ron Frehm; page 19: David Kadlubowski/AP Photo/Tampa Tribune; page 23:
Kathy Willens/AP Photo; page 25: Jim McIsaac/Getty Images; page 28: Rich Pilling/MLB Photos via
Getty Images; page 30: Mark Lennihan/AP Photo; page 33: Jamie Squire/Getty Images; page 35:
Pat Sullivan-Pool/Getty Images; page 37: Eric Risberg/AP Photo; page 38: Lou Requena/AFP/Getty
Images; page 41: Kathy Willens/AP Photo; page 43: Jonathon Gruenke/AP Photo/Kalamazoo Gazette;
page 46: Getty Images; page 47: Jim McIsaac/Getty Images

Library of Congress Control Number: 2008020697

ISBN 978-0-448-45040-7   10 9 8 7 6 5 4 3 2 1

ALL ABOARD READING™

Station Stop 3

DEREK JETER
A Yankee Hero

By B. A. Roth

with photographs

Grosset & Dunlap

Derek Jeter was under pressure. His team, the New York Yankees, was behind two games to none against the Oakland Athletics. The teams were playing for the 2001 American League title.

The Yankees, who were the 2000 World Series champs, had their title to defend. They needed to win Game 3. If they didn't, then the A's would win the title. But right now, things weren't looking so good. They were in the bottom of the seventh inning and the A's had a man on first with a chance to tie the game.

It was eighty-two degrees and clear at Network Associates Coliseum in Oakland, California. A crowd of 55,831 watched as the A's Jeremy Giambi waited on first base. The Yankees pitcher, Mike Mussina, faced batter Terrence Long. Yankees catcher Jorge Posada crouched behind home plate. The pitch was thrown. *Whack!* Long hit the ball to right field where Shane Spencer was waiting for it. Spencer picked up the ball and threw it down the first-base line toward home plate. Giambi took off. He passed second base. But the ball that Spencer threw missed first baseman Tino Martinez, who was the cutoff man. Giambi was waved past third and was heading toward home. If Giambi scored, then the score would be 1–1.

Suddenly, out of nowhere, Derek Jeter raced from his position at shortstop, grabbed the ball, and flipped it to Posada. Posada tagged the approaching Giambi. Giambi was out at the plate. Jeter had just made an unbelievable out! The move was later voted number 7 in *Baseball Weekly*'s 10 Most Amazing Plays of All Time.

The Jeter "flip" was the series turning

point for the Yankees. It gave the team
the confidence to surge ahead. Derek
and the Yankees went on to win that
game 1–0. And they came back to win
the American League Division title, three
games to two.

EARLY LIFE

Derek Sanderson Jeter was born June 26, 1974. He spent his early years in the leafy New York suburb of Pequannock, New Jersey. His parents, Charles and Dorothy Jeter, named their son after Derek Sanderson, a hockey player who led the Boston Bruins to two Stanley Cups in the 1970s.

Derek was born into a sports-crazed family. As a student at Fisk University, his father Charles Jeter had played shortstop on the varsity team. Derek's younger sister, Sharlee, was a successful basketball, softball, and volleyball athlete for her school teams. Gary Jeter, a cousin, had played football for the New York Giants.

When Derek was four, his father decided to return to school and earn a graduate degree. The family moved to Kalamazoo, Michigan, where Charles enrolled in Western Michigan University.

During the summers, Derek went back to New Jersey to stay with his mother's parents, Dot and Sonny Connors. Every morning, after his grandfather left for work, Derek would wake his grandmother and say, "Come on, Gram! Let's throw!" The two of them would play catch in the backyard. Grandma Dot was a huge Yankees fan. She used to always tell him stories of the Yankee greats—Babe Ruth, Lou Gehrig, Joe DiMaggio, Whitey Ford, and Mickey Mantle.

At age five, Derek began playing Little League baseball. Charles coached his son's team. Derek always wanted to play shortstop, but his dad challenged him to be an all-around player. If he learned to play

Two of Jeter's heroes: Yankee legends Mickey Mantle and Joe DiMaggio in 1972.

other positions, he could help his team in many ways.

With his father as coach, Derek learned important lessons. "If you're dedicated and work hard," his father said, "all your dreams will come true." Derek once told reporters, "My folks taught me that there may be people who have more talent, but there's never any excuse for anyone to work harder than you—and I believe that."

To keep the Jeter children focused on their goals, Charles and Dorothy made them sign contracts at the beginning of every school year. The contracts stated what was expected of the kids in school that year. If Derek and Sharlee met the terms of the contracts, they were rewarded.

Even though school was important to Derek, playing baseball was his life. From the age of six on, he told anyone who would listen that it was his dream to one day play shortstop for the New York Yankees. In the eighth grade, his class was given an assignment to write about what they wanted to be when they grew up. Derek wrote about playing for the Yankees in the World Series.

Derek's parents were his heroes. Mr. and Mrs. Jeter had faced many challenges as a biracial couple. But they loved each other and their family very much. Derek's parents gave him the right tools to make it in the major league and in life.

From an early age, Derek was teased by other children because his father is black and his mother is white. But his parents taught him that all people should be treated equally. The color of your skin didn't matter. He learned from his parents that if he just worked hard at his game, he would earn the respect of his classmates and teammates.

His parents may have been his personal heroes, but his sports hero was Yankee great Dave Winfield. Dave Winfield was Derek's favorite Yankee player. Derek admired the fact that Winfield was a great athlete. He was drafted in baseball, football, and

Jeter's hero, Dave Winfield, swings at a pitch in Yankee Stadium.

basketball. Derek was also impressed that Winfield started a foundation to help kids. Later, this gave Derek the inspiration to start his own charitable foundation.

Having great role models in life inspired Derek Jeter to work hard to achieve his dream of becoming a professional baseball player.

HIGH SCHOOL

In 1988, Derek entered Kalamazoo Central High School. He didn't make the varsity baseball team right away, but he quickly worked his way up the junior varsity team. His coach saw that Derek was a very talented baseball player. In fact, the coach thought he was the most talented baseball player in the entire school!

Jeter's high school coach poses with a wax figure of Jeter at Madame Tussauds.

But Derek wasn't happy just playing baseball. When the baseball season was over, he joined the school's varsity basketball team. He continued with the team through his senior year where he was the varsity captain. Playing with him on the team were Chris Webber and Jalen Rose. Those players both went on to play ball for the University of Michigan and later for the NBA.

For his senior year, Derek wanted to focus on playing baseball. But he also worked very hard on his studies, and it paid off. He was in the top ten percent of his grade and he scored high on his college entrance exams. He was also a member of the National Honor Society and head of the Latin club. Many colleges offered him scholarships. He chose the University of Michigan.

At the same time, several Major League Baseball teams were trying to recruit him. In 1992, his senior year, Derek was awarded the Kalamazoo Area B'nai B'rith Award for Scholar Athlete and the High School Player of the Year award from the American Baseball Coaches Association. He also won the 1992 Gatorade High School Athlete of the Year and *USA Today*'s High School Player of the Year.

By the end of his senior year, twenty-seven out of the twenty-eight major league teams had contacted him. They all were interested in having Derek Jeter play for them. There was only one problem—his favorite team, the New York Yankees, hadn't called!

RISE THROUGH THE MINOR LEAGUES

Derek Jeter was nervous. The MLB Draft was scheduled for June 1, 1992, and he still hadn't heard from the Yankees. Finally, a scout from the Yankees named Dick Groch called Derek to say his team was interested and that they were probably going to call. All Derek had to do was be patient.

Jeter wins the Rookie of the Year Award in 1996.

Since the baseball draft is not televised, Derek did not know what was happening. Would he get drafted? And by which team? Finally, the phone rang. The Yankees wanted to make him an offer! Derek spoke to Gene Michael, the Yankees' general manager. Michael told Derek that the team had great hopes and expectations for him.

A few days after he turned eighteen, Derek and his father negotiated a contract with the Yankees worth $800,000 plus a $700,000 signing bonus. In addition, the Yankees agreed to pay for Derek's tuition at the University of Michigan so that during the off-season while he played in the minors, Derek could attend school. He did attend some classes, but he never graduated from college. On June 28, 1992, Derek signed the contract with the

Yankees. He was the first high-school student to be chosen by the Yankees in the 1992 draft.

Two days later, he headed to Tampa, Florida, for spring training in the Gulf Coast Rookie League. Michael had plans for Derek to spend several years training with minor league teams. Even though Derek came to the Yankees with a great record, they didn't want to rush him through the system. They wanted to bring him up slowly.

The minor leagues are also known as the "farm system." It is set up so that each major league baseball team can have their new recruits train and play against other players at the same level. The minor league teams ranked as A, AA, and AAA. And each major league team may have more than one minor league team.

AAA is more competitive than A. The Yankees have all three levels of minor league teams. They have an A team in Greensboro, North Carolina. Their AA team is in Albany, New York. And their AAA team is in Columbus, Ohio.

Derek had never been away from home before, and it took some getting used to. For the first time, he had to learn how to live by himself. He cleaned his own clothes and cooked his own food. He missed his family very much and spent

Yankees owner George Steinbrenner watches his Gulf Coast League rookie team.

many hours on the phone to either Mom or Dad.

Derek was playing baseball, but he was frustrated. Even though he was the number-two draft selection, he faced a lot of competition from the other players in the league. Back in high school he had an unheard-of batting average of .557. Yet, in his first year in the minor leagues, his average was just .202.

The next year was better for Derek. He moved up to the Class A Greensboro team. He started as shortstop. But he still struggled, making fifty-six errors during that season. The Yankees told him not to worry. They still believed in him.

On the hitting side, Derek was doing well. He batted .295 with five home runs, seventy-one RBIs, and eighteen stolen bases. He was voted "Most Outstanding

Major League Prospect" by South Atlantic League managers. The minor league-based magazine, *Baseball America*, crowned him the "Most Exciting Player" and "Best Infield Arm" in the minors.

June 1994 was a great month for Derek. He was rewarded with a promotion to the Yankees' AA Team in Albany. There, he posted an impressive .377 batting average. In August, he moved up to play AAA with the Columbus Clippers.

After the 1994 season, Derek Jeter was named the Minor League Player of the Year by *Baseball America*, *Sporting News*, *USA Today Baseball Weekly*, and Topps/NAPBL. Now Jeter had one more goal to achieve—to make it to the major league as a New York Yankees player.

YANKEE AT LAST

On May 28, 1995, the phone rang
in the Jeter household in Kalamazoo,
Michigan. It was the Yankees home office.
Their star shortstop, Tony Fernandez, was
injured and his backup, Rudy Velarde,
was needed at second base. The Yankees
were in a tight spot. They needed help.
They needed someone good. Derek was
their man.

Before he knew it, he was boarding
a plane to join the team for their May 29
game against the Seattle Mariners. When
he got to the visitors' locker room at the
Kingdome in Seattle, he found his number
2 away uniform waiting for him.

Derek's fieldwork was perfect but
he was unable to get even one hit. The
Yankees ended up losing to the Mariners

Derek Jeter shares a hug with his father before the start of a game on Father's Day.

by a score of 8–7. The Mariners won the next game, too, 7–2. This time, Derek made two hits, scoring both times. After the game, Derek and his dad went to a local McDonald's to celebrate his good playing!

The team traveled back to Yankee Stadium for Derek's New York debut against the California Angels. Derek's entire family showed up to cheer him on. He was thrilled to be in New York and to be a part of the Yankees. Although the team lost that game, Jeter played a great defensive game.

Tony Fernandez soon recovered and Jeter was sent back down to Columbus after playing only a few games in the major league. The Yankees' season ended by losing the American League Division title to the Mariners, three games to two.

The owner of the Yankees, George Steinbrenner, was frustrated. He wanted a World Series championship. He fired manager Buck Showalter and hired former player and coach Joe Torre to manage the team.

Steinbrenner also wanted to bring Jeter back to New York. Torre didn't think Jeter was ready. But when Fernandez became injured again, they needed Derek back.

Torre admired Derek's dedication to the team. He liked Jeter's athletic ability and people skills. Jeter respected Torre, too.

Jeter was the first rookie to start as a Yankees shortstop since 1962. Some critics thought he wouldn't be able to take the pressure. But he proved them wrong. Jeter was unique because he was great in the field *and* at bat. He had a .314/.370/.430 average (that's batting average/on base percentage/slugging

Joe Torre and Derek Jeter look on in the ninth inning against Boston.

percentage) during the regular season. In the postseason, he had a .415/.415/.561 average. He also had ten home runs, seventy-eight RBIs, and fourteen steals.

Derek started off the season by scoring his first home run, helping to defeat the Cleveland Indians 7–1. He ended the season by helping his team capture the American League Championship (ALCS) title by defeating the Baltimore Orioles four games to one. In one of the games against the Orioles, a fourteen-year-old fan named Jeffrey Maier snagged one of Jeter's home-run balls. But Orioles right fielder Tony Tarasco thought that he should have been able to catch the ball. He wanted an interference call. The ump called it a home run, tying up the score. New York went on to win the game 5–4. Later, they moved on to play defending Series champs, the Atlanta Braves, for the World Series title.

Most critics and fans predicted that the Braves would beat the Yankees. The Yanks lost their first two games at home. Miraculously, the Yanks won the next two with a come-from-behind rally in Game 4. They ended up defeating the Braves four games to two. The Yankees had accomplished George Steinbrenner's dream of bringing the title back to Yankee Stadium for the first time since 1978. All of New York City was cheering. The mayor of New York City, Rudy Giuliani, ordered a ticker-tape parade for New York's heroes.

For Derek, it was his best year ever. He had posted some incredible stats and was voted Rookie of the Year. Plus, he had just won his first World Series ring. The fans began to notice this new, young player. Derek enjoyed his new popularity, but he also knew that he had to work hard on the field. In the 1997 season, Torre moved him from a batting position of ninth to the leadoff man.

The 1997 season ended with an extremely close division series with Cleveland. Jeter even hit an incredible home run that saved Game 2. But in the tie-breaking fifth game, the Yanks fell apart and lost, three games to two.

MOST VALUABLE PLAYER

The Yankees had a shaky start in 1998. They lost three straight games in April. This hadn't happened to the team in thirteen years! But on May 17, pitcher David Wells completed a "perfect game." A perfect game is when the same pitcher plays throughout an entire game without letting the opposing team reach first base. He was only the fifteenth pitcher ever to complete a perfect game. Many people said that game was a turning point in the Yankees' season.

Derek Jeter was having a good season, too. He made his first appearance (as a reserve) in the All-Star game on July 7. The Yanks went on to beat the Cleveland Indians four games to two for the American League East title. And then they swept the San Diego Padres four games to zero in the World Series. The team had improved their overall record to 125-50. Again, New York City treated them to a ticker-tape parade. Derek ended up .324/.384/.481, with 127 runs.

When the 1999 season rolled around, George Steinbrenner decided to make some changes. The change that upset

New York City celebrates with a ticker-tape parade.

the fans the most was when he traded star pitcher David Wells and two other players to the Toronto Blue Jays for ace pitcher Roger Clemens.

But for Derek, things were looking good. He was now twenty-five years old and had just re-signed with the team for a contract worth $4 million. Halfway through the season he led the league in all batting stats. And it looked like he was going to beat his nineteen home runs from '98. Torre also put Derek in the third batting spot.

When it came to the All-Star game, it seemed certain that Derek would be named the starting shortstop. But Boston's short-stop, Nomar Garciaparra, was also having a good year. And he won the starting spot.

The All-Star game is a popularity contest. The players are voted on by the fans. Using the Internet, fans are allowed to each vote twenty-five times. The week before the votes were counted, Garciaparra trailed Jeter by about thirty thousand votes. Jeter lost to Garciaparra by about twenty thousand votes. What happened? It was later discovered that a student at the Massachusetts Institute of Technology had hacked into the program that counted the votes, and voted forty thousand times for his favorite Boston shortstop. Joe Torre, who was the American League manager for the All-Stars, placed Jeter on the team as backup.

The Yankees played well that season. And in Game 5 of the American League East championship against Boston, it was Jeter's turn to shine. He clobbered a two-run homer early on in the game. After that, the Sox fell apart and the Yankees finished the series, winning four games to one. The Yanks moved on to the World Series to face the Atlanta Braves again.

The media was calling the Yankees the "Team of the Century." They had twenty-four World Series titles. And with the year 2000 coming up, it seemed as if they would also take the title "Team of the Decade."

Jeter jumps into the air to celebrate a home run in Game 4 of the World Series.

But the Braves were a tough team. It would be hard to beat them this year. The Braves pitchers—Greg Maddux, John Smoltz, John Rocker, and Tom Glavine—and power hitters—Chipper Jones, Andruw Jones, and Bret Boone—were on fire. Jeter came into the series ready to play. He had two hits in each of the first two World Series games. And he ended the series batting .353.

The Yankees beat Atlanta four games to one. They were now truly both the "Team of the Century" *and* "Team of the Decade." And for Derek Jeter, this was his second World Series ring.

The Yankees, however, did not start off well the next season. By the end of June, the team was only 38-36. In the last week of that month the Yankees lost their last seven games. The Yankees, and their

fans, were not happy.

But things were looking up for Jeter. Once again, he was named to the American League All-Star team. Derek ended up winning the All-Star game's MVP (Most Valuable Player) award. He was the first Yankee to win the award since it was given out in 1962!

Then things began to turn around for the Yankees. They made it into the World Series to face the New York Mets. This exciting series, known as the Subway Series, caused New York sports fans to go wild! The Yankees took the first game by a score of 4–3 in twelve innings. And they won the second game 6–5. The Mets came back to win Game 3 by a score of 4–2.

Game 4 started off with a bang as Derek Jeter clobbered the first pitch from Bobby Jones for a homer. The Yanks held the score at 3–2 early on and until the game ended. The Yanks took Game 5, and another World Series title. Derek ended the year with a .339/.416/.481 average. He also won the MVP award for the series.

Derek Jeter proved to be a key defensive player for the Yankees in the

2001 American League championship series. Game 3 against the Oakland Athletics was a must-win for the Yankees. They were down in the series two games to none. In that game, Jeter's now-famous "flip" to Jorge Posada helped keep the Yankees' 1–0 lead. They went on to win the game.

In Game 5 of the series, the Yankees held a 5–3 lead. At the top of the eighth, Jeter went for a foul ball hit by Terrence

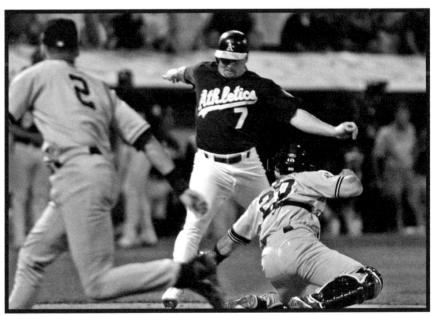

Jeter's famous "flip" gets Giambi out at home plate.

Long. He ran to the stands, looked
quickly, jumped in, and grabbed the ball!
The Yankees won the game and the series.

In the 2001 World Series, the Yankees
faced the Arizona Diamondbacks. In Game
4, the Yanks were down one game to two
in the series. Once again, they needed a
win to stay in the race. And once again,
Derek would come through for his team.
His home run in the eighth inning tied

the series at two games apiece. The media and the fans considered Jeter a hero. In fact, he was given the nickname "Mr. November." (The World Series was played in November that year.)

However, the season wrapped up for the Yankees in Game 7. It was the bottom of the ninth inning. A Diamondback fly ball went over Derek's head, scoring the winning run. In spite of his team's loss, Derek had a great season. He earned twenty-one home runs, twenty-seven stolen bases, and batted .311/.377/.480 and .444/.474/.500 in the postseason.

The 2002 season marked the Yankees' 100th anniversary as a New York baseball team. And even though the team lost three great players that year—Paul O'Neill, Tino Martinez, and Chuck Knoblauch—the team finished the regular season on top in the American League, 103-58. But the Yanks did not get far in the postseason. They lost the American League title to the Anaheim Angels, four games to one. This would be the first time since 1997 that the Yankees wouldn't go to the World Series. For Derek Jeter, it was the first time in five years that he hadn't been nominated for MVP.

The 2003 season opened with a disaster for Jeter in the game with the Toronto Blue Jays. Derek ran into a runner and dislocated his arm. He was on the disabled list for thirty-six games.

But then Jeter got some good news. On June 3, 2003, Derek Jeter became the eleventh team captain in Yankees history. Not since Don Mattingly left the team in 1995 had the team had a captain. George Steinbrenner was the only person who

Former team captain Don Mattingly poses with current team captain Derek Jeter.

could name captains, and he had been thinking about appointing Derek for many years. Now that he had been named captain, Jeter had a lot of responsibility.

The Yankees finished the season with a record of 101-61. But they ended up losing the World Series that year to the Florida Marlins, four games to two. The Yankees and their fans were crushed by the loss. But Jeter still had a great year with batting stats of .324/.393/.450.

JETER STYLE

Derek Jeter worked hard during the baseball season. But he also enjoyed going out and having a good time. It seemed that whenever someone opened up a magazine, Derek was there. Not only was he in *Sports Illustrated*, but he was also seen in *GQ, Cosmopolitan*, and many teen magazines.

But even though he was popular with his fans, Derek had a good work ethic. He stayed focused. He knew right from wrong. And he was grateful for all that he had. His parents had taught him how important it was to help others. So Derek formed the Turn 2 Foundation. In baseball, the term "turn two" is a reference to a double play.

Derek started the Turn 2 Foundation

in 1996. The foundation supports athletic kids in western Michigan and the New York metropolitan area. It helps to run baseball clinics and leadership and youth groups. Turn 2 also gives school scholarships. As president of the foundation, Jeter has created many programs himself. With the help of his agent, father, mother, and sister—all of whom help run the foundation—Turn 2 has become a success.

Derek Jeter smiles at a gathering for participants in the Turn 2 Foundation.

ALWAYS A CHAMP

The 2004 season was not going well for Derek or the Yankees. He came out of a serious hitting slump in April after going 0-32 and batting .161. No one, not even his coach, manager, or fellow teammates, could figure out what the problem was.

Then, on July 1, 2004, Jeter made a great defensive play. In the twelfth inning of a tie-game against the Boston Red Sox, Boston's Trot Nixon hit a pop-up down the left-field line. Jeter sprinted for the ball from his position at shortstop. He made a running catch at full-speed, sending him into the stands headfirst. Jeter held on to the ball. But when he came out from the stands, he was bruised and bloodied. He had to leave the game for X-rays. But Jeter rejoined the lineup the next night against the New York Mets.

Derek finished the 2004 season with a .292 average. He had twenty-three home runs, the third most of his career. He also had forty-four doubles. That record earned him the Hank Aaron Award. That award is given to the player with the best overall hitting record in the league.

But best of all, Jeter won the Golden Glove Award. The award is given to the player judged by MLB managers and coaches to have been the best fielder that year. Derek Jeter was the first Yankee shortstop to earn the award.

In 2005, the Yankees spent most of the season chasing the 2004 World Series champs, the Boston Red Sox, for the AL division title. But they ended up losing to the L.A. Angels of Anaheim 3–2.

Jeter jumps to make a catch against the Boston Red Sox.

From 2005 to 2007, Derek continued to keep over a .300 batting average. He made more than two hundred hits and made the MVP list each year. Although his team has not won a pennant title since 2003, Derek continues to lead and inspire the Yankees. He has shown his loyalty throughout sixteen years of commitment to the team. This is the team he had always dreamed he would be a part of some day.

Derek Jeter always practices hard. And he is always focused on his goals. Derek has always made his team, and his fans, proud. Perhaps that is why, on August 25, 2007, voters named Derek Jeter the "Face of the Yankees."

Derek Jeter's 2008 Records

★ Jeter batted .300 with 179 hits and 11 home runs in the 2008 season.

★ In June 2008, Jeter hit his 400th double at Yankee Stadium.

★ In July 2008, Jeter hit his 200th career home run.

★ In August 2008, Jeter reached a career milestone with 2,500 hits.

★ On September 16, Jeter surpassed Lou Gehrig as the player with the most hits in Yankee Stadium, with 1,270!

★ Jeter was selected to be on the American League's All-Star team for the ninth time in his career, and played as the starting short stop.

Derek Jeter's Career Highlights

★ Jeter was named All-Star Game MVP and World Series MVP in the same season in 2000.

★ Jeter was named the 11th captain of the Yankees in 2003. He was the first player to be named captain since Don Mattingly retired in 1995!

★ Jeter won Gold Gloves in 2004, 2005, and 2006.

★ Jeter has over 1,000 career RBIs.